The author has a dream. The dream is love, not greed. So he has written poems for over 50 years. He cherishes himself, his people, his society. They are the foundation of his poetry.

Dedicated to my family, neighbors, and loved ones passing by.

Yonah Jeong

THE ISLANDS ARE NOT LONELY

AUSTIN MACAULEY PUBLISHERS™

LONDON • CAMBRIDGE • NEW YORK • SHARJAH

Ordering Information
Quantity sales: Special discounts are available on quantity purchases by corporations, associations, and others. For details, contact the publisher at the address below.

Publisher's Cataloging-in-Publication data
Jeong, Yonah
The Islands Are Not Lonely

ISBN 9781638294795 (Paperback)
ISBN 9781638294801 (Hardback)
ISBN 9781638294825 (ePub e-book)
ISBN 9781638294818 (Audiobook)

Library of Congress Control Number: 2023901100

www.austinmacauley.com/us

First Published 2023
Austin Macauley Publishers LLC
40 Wall Street, 33rd Floor, Suite 3302
New York, NY 10005
USA

mail-usa@austinmacauley.com
+1 (646) 5125767

Austin Macauley Publishers, friends, books.

1. By the Power of Unemployment

A good man
holding the address found
in the weekly newsletter
went to the nursing home
with only grandmothers
grandma's painful place
searching this and that
the friendly stories
massage
knead
had fun together
the enemployed man was saying
"take off the rings"
"blood circulation is good"
about ring was given by someone
the grandma's pride satisfied
times went by
when grandma's heart
relaxed
forgot the ring

the young man took them
ran away.

2. Absolute Proposition

Mother
is
not
enough

Maternal love
is
not
lacking.

3. On Integration

In this world

left eye and right eye
left shoulder and right shoulder
left hand and right hand
left ear and right ear
left knee and right knee
left foot and right foot
left brain and right brain

move and role
each other
different

here is a heart.

It is on the left
but
people don't call it
left heart.

4. Spring Rain

Spring rains...spring rains
man of mood chatterbox

spring coming...spring hearing
falling or soaking

pushing up moist
let the sprouts say "Hi!"

5. Sacrifice

Gathering
all the money
buy tickets

Enter

One
two
waiting songs
the great orchestra
melodies
conductor, back view

Roasted the peanut flavor

Cannot breathe
also eyes
fall into hearing
invisible next seat
by the way
crying of a hidden child
hug a hilarious

learned and decent eyes
focus on this moment

On the stage
the dancing baton
stops
and
mother becomes mom
goes out of the curtain

About 10 seconds

Mom becomes mother
comes inside the curtain

the music comes back to life.

6. Spring in the Winter

The spring was not
in the flower

People
play with
it is fun

It was spring in winter
winter always hid
in stacked snow

Clearing snow piles
let the streets get clean
can't catch anyone's eyes
winter
covered with heavy dusts
now spring of the snow
has coming

Here or there
to welcome us.

7. Marriage Life

At early honeymoon
quietly
sleeping with closed the mouth
you were beautiful

After 30 years
snoring
sleeping with open the mouth
you are so beautiful

The meaningful marriage
life
is to prove love each other.

8. Meeting Place

The sea
seaside of sands
lies on the bed of small stones
look up the sky
there is another sea
it shows me
clouds fishes go by
gulls fly
someone
going by boat
just stop
with a plop
the splash in water
water drops fall
after washing the face
where two seas meet
I see there.

9. A Way Station

Be
or
none
passengers who wait for

Run

someday
upon arrival
at the terminal
put all stories down
joy of meeting
sorrow of separating
in the bosom

Run

crossing
around waving river
blue heaven
green mountains

Run

while running
train thinks
a way station

stepping in
shakes white handkerchief
after few minutes
the time to leave
sweetheart
cannot meet
never again

breaking up
a lover chest
the train run.

10. About Birth

There is no
accidental
birth

There is one
essential
birth.

11. My Young Wife

Wakes up
from sleeping

Through the window
look at the morning
piled in the dark

Shouldn't doze up
while working
how hard is work!

The winding road to the home
have storm cone
should arrive very well…

Didn't give enough
pocket money

Emily Plath
married daughter

Always

be happy and healthy
like your mother.

12. Morning Coffee

put
coffee beans

close
the cover

grinding

crushing
powdering

a scent

shattering shouts
like a shadow

will be
with me

all day long
to be broken.

13. A Truth

Only one thing
that
all machines
cannot
do

A pianist
non-repeating
training
training
training.

14. One Word

Not to play
sets to play
for sixty years
sitting down before the piano

Tuning is
compromising
between rising and falling

A note can't be sound
without neighboring notes

Do not know this
player's discontents
for the piano and the audience
wining by breathtaking tuning
a tuner is loved
with the piano

For the best performance of the players
"Bravo" from the auditorium
standing backstage

have the appointment
tomorrow tuning

"Worth doing."

15. Yellow Butterfly
White Butterfly

Freedom,
eraser
to erase wrong acts
upholding equality

Shouting
pencil,
put it on the head
records and draws

In the note
yellow butterflies
white butterflies

Come from it
beyond
flower garden
fence
toward the streets
with two wings
larger than the body

Do not just stay
in the flower bed
ignoring
the traffic light

Fly.

16. A Wallet Is Crying

Busily
from NJ to NY coming and going
meet G. W. Bridge
at entrance to New Jersey
sometimes encounter
a mid-30s female

She can't holding a light paper
words of desperate help
by the spring breeze
drops and picks up
over and over
when bows down
hot afternoon sun
pours behind back

Hurriedly
I take out my wallet
lower window a little
hand over one dollar

She blesses my future
never forgets to smile

As soon as
I do that
unbearable sorrows coming out
my fingers begin to tremble.

17. Because of Love

An aged boy
is wonder
wakes up at the dawn
secretly
looks through the house
neighborhood backstreets
market stores

Walks around and takes a look
the light is invisible

Goes up and down the back garden

Meeting animals
smiling flowers
whispering streams
shiny pebbles
a rocking sea
dancing grass
blowing winds

Cannot see the light
dragging a tired body
in hopelessness
opens the bedroom door in warehouse
sleeps like the dead
crying in the nightmare
opens eyes slowly
light comes through the gaps of the door
touches the lip

The light was in the darkness.

18. Worm

To avoid
overlapping summer heat
into the mosquito net
gathered together
as soon as sit down
pieces of peach
come in
with a white plate

Each other
put in the mouth
talk what happened day

Suddenly
"No?
It's a bug."
"Hey!
peach eaten by the worm
more delicious
is good
there is a little pesticide."

From the side
the sound of a mosquito
worm whispers

"The same for people."

19. Wolf!

01/13/2021

People surprised
'Wolf is coming'
whole town
panic

People paid attention to
enjoyed lying
the shepherd boy

One day
appeared
boy ran like a cheetah
toward the town plaza
falling and falling
shouted

"Wolves!"
nobody paid attention

What happened
to a shepherd boy and his sheep?
the answer
in today paper.

20. New Year Wishes

A sharp sunlight
the frozen fresh air
comes down to the roof leisurely
and stuck on the wall with the spider
the surprised child
with the curious eyes
put face at the window
kisses
eye for eye
tooth for tooth
last year
spent with longing
with greater loving
by melting frozen sunlight
on the Harlem Street
on the old malt railroad
on the cracked cement
on the alleyway
in the flooded neighborhood
and the wall street stores
cow weeping
calm moonshine

in the evening
will knocks your home.

21. Hunter

Work
for eating
eat
for working

No

for working
for eating

We cannot eat
anymore
sure know
throw away
daily
useless things
like the discarded garbage
trapped the big barrier of LSD
in the Wall Street

Money gives us the trouble of the money

Poetry: the solution of the money

The poem hunter
Fighting for the poems
instead of stock prices.

22. I Am a Son

My parent
ninety years old
they live from
the foreign country
when
calling
sending text message
paper letter
also
when they have something to
ask
seek consultant
give and take
the affectionate tales
choose
with daughter-in-law
not me

I like it better.

23. A Tree

A tree
Celsius -10 degrees
winter nights
on the side of the asphalt road
standing

Too many cars
passing by
no one
keep eyes on

By the light
becomes a red tree
when snow accumulates
be
white tree branches
hairs
of the old tree

As the close friend
three guys
stop one way no left turn

a loner
do not enter

A winter tree
stepped on countless times
with the shadow which doesn't tear
by luxury police construction cars
thinks and looks at

A coming spring
along the street.

24. Curtain and Window

Curtain
do not show

Window
do not hide

Just curtain and window meet
the fight game happens
when the window wins
spring and summer form
when curtain overcomes
autumn and winter occur

Win-Win
makes the peace
four seasons
a life.

25. Mirror and Window

When the winter comes
wind blows strong
a step accelerates
closes doors
seeing myself
before the mirror
in the mood of
cold and shriveled

When the spring comes
in the offish air
wind blows still
a step slows
opens the door
seeing neighbors
through the window.

26. The Wings of Imagination

Knock three times
knock
knock
knock

Who?
no one
coming here

Wind
a deer family
moonlight
broken branches of the tree
auditory
hallucination

As soon as
I see it
becomes the melody
cross the mountains
with me.

27. A Song for Winter

Night
winter
wine
in a glass

Why?

Around the evening
heart beats fast
head moves slowly
body dozes temperately

At small village
winter
comes closer

snowing building scattering
forest
wind blows
between these things all

For few years of winter
night gives light
it is the sound of dropping water
it is from red handkerchief to white carpet
it is neither noisy nor quiet
like the breaking branches
with foresight

A seed of the change raises head
without words

This moment
is the evening of the winter.

28. Daniel

Can't go anymore
gathering in the lowest place
the water becomes the sea

Pacific
Indian
East, not the Sea of Japan
Mediterranean
Caribbean
Gulf

The sea is not overflowing
there is no shortage

The sea embraces in the breast
rivers
even if bullied
do not a face to face
it makes the beach

Like
twelve months Daniel

slick, slick, slick
smiles.

29. Wanna Be

You
keep me away

Selfish
not knowing how to love
saying nonsense
staying
without politeness

At somewhere invisible
not by your side
I call you
songs
whispering
of the flowing brook in the rocks
covered with trees

I gesture
can't run to you
can't talk to you

I wanna be stay
even on the face
the dragonfly sunglasses.

30. Wisdom

To listen
is
to understand

To speak
is
to judge.

31. Humble and Proud

The rabbit
forgets the turtle
thinks about victory

In fact
knows well
rabbit cannot lose in the race

The turtle
remembers the rabbit
think about defeat

In fact
knows well
turtle cannot win in the race

Whose side is the victory on?

32. My Grandaunt

When I leave the rural house
in the countryside
Grandaunt gives me bus fee
"When you were a little
carrying you on my back
went around alleys of village
now…"
Grandaunt beckons
"Go quickly"
for a while
walk along
the footpath between rice fields
stop and look back
still standing
leaning on the shabby fence
she looks at me
several times
I would go back her bosom
but just
cross the front small mountain.

33. My Love

When
I write poems
with arguments
for philosophy
my love
knows
how to love me
she gets torn back of hand
exhaustion
wears old working uniform
since last summer
meets the lonely night
in snowing

My love
makes my poetry.

34. Morning Greetings

Morning
brings
a trace of the deep night

Wake up
to see the sky
open the window
the fence of
the front house
to touch
bare branches of
dozens of old rivers
I reach out my hands

Soon

Hand meddling fragment clouds
…holding floating stars
…bending a universe

Morning
presenting
a little peace.

35. Modern Love

A shopping list
-----steel head
-----pomegranate
-----sweet onion
-----org onion
-----bananas
-----short ribs
go in with the cart
look around here and there
get what I need
pay money
exit
open rear door of the car
put inside things
slowly
down the door
pushing a cart into the storage
getting in
moves
toward uneasy house.

36. From View to Hope

Now
the winds blow
clouds in the hazy sky
think
it will be weeping
at the Apt. edge
leaves hanging on the back
of the Ginko branch
struck
like to gall
in the hallway
puppy barking
a child's eyes
footprints
washing machine running
sink…dripping water
go through the crack window
shake
maple trees
touch
so that it is not cold
during the night

views of fall disappear
through the morning sun
those became a hope.

37. On Someone's Cheek

Terrified
New York
Greenwich village

Hundreds of millions
snows are falling

From the last night
pour out without getting tired

Until I see it
concrete floor
put it away
looking back up
as stacking up again
morning to evening

From the high and wide sky
to this low and narrow place
without a break
thousands of miles
running down

Let's touch snowflakes
on my cheek
it just tickle

Sit down on my eyebrows
not heavy
in the blink of eyes
disappear
becoming teardrops
but not sad

I wanna be reach to you
like that.

38. Waiting

Where
does it come from?

Magnolia flowers
between old-fashioned buildings
quiet lane
a bench by the river
taxi passenger humming
coming with?

Street corner
poor shop
door opening sound
along the bicycle wheels
traffic light and signs
coming with?

No
spring doesn't come that way

Resting on the chest
looking at baby daughter

following the mother's gaze
it was already there.

39. When a Sparrow
Flew Away From

Going down Apt. stairs
saw a dozing sparrow by the window
held down
a sparrow escaped to upstairs rooftop
but hit beak to an iron door and
be shut in the corner
pressed a sparrow with flat bag softly
left hand grabbed and caught
with proud emotion
to bus station
walked in deep thoughts

Fly a night
when the morning comes
will ask mother then forcibly
will tie a sparrow ankle with thread sturdy
from yard to rice paddies and an empty field
a grandson will scamper

While I felt so good
my right fingers relaxed

flapping
opened wings powerful
circled around top of an electric pole
a sparrow grew
farther and farther
away

a piece of my dream.

40. A Traffic Light

Drive carefully
slightly frozen the way
cross Hackensack River bridge
pass the neighborhood
run the factory road
see the looming light
from a distance
at the moment
thoughts go back to the old days

For nearly forty years
my friend treated me with smiling
even while fighting
reconciled
I couldn't feel friend's pains
I believed
he didn't have any sufferings
even when we separated
I only made the judgment
I did not try to understand
I was such a friend

I can call friend's name
I can't see him again but
I see his face
in water drops
among the scattered snowflakes
in the storm wind
laughing
is washed by the wiper

As I look up
by the cracking sound
a traffic light changed
already.

41. Dart

On the room door
toward dartboard
one
two
three
threw arrow
singly
even if I threw
dozens of times
I couldn't hit
the center spot
so
I pictured a hating face
There and
shot
last left arrow
hit
a perfect score!

42. How Good Would It Be

The car
is moving backwards
with the warning sound
to the danger
"for Elise"

I surprised

The poet
can play such a role
in the society
if there is such a beauty
"warning sign."

43. Poem's Run

Poem
in the early morning

Juice
omelet
orange
steak
forks and knives
on shaking old table
with jazz melodies
it becomes a meal

A waitress
cleaning side seat
scenery outside window
it comes into the glass of wine

Riding on a look
afternoon sun
winds
going through the long tunnel of the night
the heartbroken world

73

Poem
in the "good morning."

44. Love 2

With cold from far
a shivering tree

Can you give
warm water?

CPSIA information can be obtained
at www.ICGtesting.com
Printed in the USA
BVHW050950060423
661865BV00002B/99